Pet Loss and Helping Your Child Cope with the Loss of a Pet

By Erainna Winnett, Ed. S.

Counseling with HEART Books

Counselingwithheart.com

Pet Loss and Children: Helping Your Child Cope with the Loss of a Pet
Text © 2014 Erainna Winnett
Cover Design Chamillah Designs
Interior Layout Carii Designs

All rights reserved. No part of this book may be reproduced or transmitted in any form or by any means, electronic or mechanical, including photocopying, recording, or by an information storage retrieval system, without permission in writing from the publisher, except for brief quotations for critical reviews.

Library of Congress: Cataloging-in-Publication Data
Winnett, Erainna
Pet Loss and Children: Helping Your Child Cope with the Loss of a Pet
1. Pet Loss – Bereavement 2. Pet Loss – Mourning
3. Parenting – Death and Grief
4. Children – Sadness

ISBN-13: 978-0692310908
ISBN-10: 0692310908

Printed in the United States of America

10 9 8 7 6 5 4 3 2 1

DEDICATION

*To our best friends, who may have paws,
whiskers, scales, fins, feathers, fur, or a beak.*

*When you touched our hearts,
you became a part of our soul.*

"If there is a heaven, it's certain our animals are to be there. Their lives become so interwoven with our own, it would take more than an archangel to detangle them."

- Pam Brown, Australian poet

What parents are saying about *Pet Loss and Children*…

"I had never given much thought about children mourning until the unexpected death of a fluffy little kitten we had named Riff. My granddaughter didn't seem to be terribly upset but she was unusually quiet and withdrawn. I found *Pet Loss and Children* to give me some insight into how children grieve when they experience the loss of a pet. I highly recommend this book to anyone who has a pet because even though it is sad, our dear pets do not live as long as people." ~Jenny Chandelier

"For every child who loses a pet this is an amazing story for helping your kids grieve the loss of their pet. I remember when I was a little girl I lost a couple of foals. No one helped me through it and I wish I had had this book to read with my mom." ~Betty J. Lloyd

AUTHOR'S RECOMMENDATION

MEMORIES OF YOU
Pet Memory Book

Few people get through childhood without experiencing the loss of a precious pet. Memories of You is an interactive memory book that honors the special role a pet plays in a child's life, from playmate to best friend to treasured source of comfort during hard times. Writing, drawing, storytelling, and other engaging exercises support children in commemorating the bond they shared with their pet from the day it entered their life. Additional activities include learning how to respond to unhelpful statements from others and planning a special service to remember a beloved pet. Children, as well as the adults who support them, will acquire a wealth of tools to process the loss of a pet with wisdom, compassion, and sweet memories to last a lifetime. Available at online bookstores.

TABLE OF CONTENTS

Introduction - How to Help Your Child Cope with Pet Loss 1

When Tears Take Over: Dealing with the Emotions of Pet Loss 5

Across the Ages: How Pet Loss Impacts Children During Their Young Lives 12

Is the Sky Blue Because I'm Sad? Questions Children May Ask about Pet Loss 22

Dear Teacher, Susie's Pet Passed: Who Needs to be Informed When Your Child Mourns 28

Mommy, I Drew a Picture: Ways to Involve Children in Pet Memorials 32

Muffin's Gone! When to Move On? 37

Conclusion 42

10 Most Asked Questions When Dealing With Pet Loss 43

Meet The Author 51

INTRODUCTION

HOW TO HELP YOUR CHILD COPE WITH PET LOSS

Everyone deals with grief differently, and children are no exception. Some cry for weeks, while others write poems or draw pictures. A child should never feel as though they can't express their emotions about losing a pet. My objective in writing this book is to help you help your child ease their pain while processing the loss of their pet.

The first thing to remember is grieving *is* a process. There's no instant way to lessen or stop the pain. An animal is a family member, and each pet plays a different role in our lives. If you feel like crying, cry; even in front of your children. Children need to see you grieve. If you cry, children know it's okay for them to cry. It can help your family feel more comfortable with the natural process of grieving.

Second, as a family, you'll need to discover how to honor your pet's memory. Several choices include: (1) Have a memorial service that gives everyone the opportunity to express their feelings and say their goodbyes. (2) Dedicate a section of the house to your pet as a memorial. (3) Have a pet funeral with a more familiar form to allow children to say their goodbyes. Involve your children as much as possible. Let them remember their pet the way they most identified with it. Remember, this is an occasion that brings the family together.

Next, you should find a support system. Your family can be your best support, because you are grieving the loss together. I recommend purchasing a pet memory book, one that will allow children to process their pain and reflect on the many happy memories they shared with their pet friend. I've written one specifically for children, but even if you decide not to purchase this one, please consider getting your child something to help comfort them. *Memories of You: Pet Memory Book* is available at online book stores.

Last, let life happen. Try to go back to your normal routine. If you are considering another pet, make sure you are ready. You do not want to take on this responsibility if you can't give the new pet the love that *every* pet deserves.

WHEN TEARS TAKE OVER: DEALING WITH THE EMOTIONS OF PET LOSS

Preparing for or dealing with the loss of a family pet is a difficult time for animal lovers of all ages. For the youngest members of your family – your children – the passing of their cat, dog, fish, bird, or reptile can bring forth so many confusing emotions that they simply have not had the life experience to understand. While you can appreciate that the loss of a pet is part of the natural course of life, a child who has not often experienced death prior to pet loss is learning these realities for the first time.

If your family has a pet that is injured or ill and you are left with no other choice but to end its suffering through euthanasia, take some time to talk with your child beforehand – preferably away from the pet to spare its emotions, as well as your child's.

Explain in a calm, soft, loving voice that the pet is in pain and will no longer suffer. Very young children do not have the emotional capabilities to fully grasp death and loss, so explaining what is happening in simple terms without a lot of details will suffice. On the other hand, older children have a better comprehension of the world around them. These children more easily read other's thoughts and feelings. For these children, the emotional toll of a pet's impending death and loss can lead to a longer time of mourning. This is especially true in older children who often view their pets as friends or whose first form of responsibility was taking care of their pet. The emotions from knowing that piece of their young lives is gone can be challenging.

Children in mourning may act out in a way that goes against their normal behaviors. They may withdraw completely, show aggression, or fall somewhere in between the two extremes. They also may worry that another family member may die because their beloved pet has. Grief-stricken children may resort to resuming habits once removed (thumb sucking or nail biting), or they may try to bargain with the death to prevent or change the outcome (e.g., I'll clean my room every day for the rest of my life if it will bring Fluffy back). Older children (10 and up) have a better grasp of life and death, but that does not change their feelings about a loss. Children with a longer bond with their pet are more likely to experience the traditional grief and mourning mechanisms that adults face as reality – feelings of loss, remorse, grief, denial, anger, guilt, and over time, acceptance. However, unlike adults, children often take longer to go through the traditional stages of grief than adults because the emotions stirred from a pet's passing are feelings that children are not used to experiencing. If your child is school-aged, it is important that you speak with his or her teachers about the loss. Your child's educators may see signs and symptoms of aggression or depression that you may not see. Letting school staffers know will help them to assist your child should sadness and other emotions, such as misdirected anger, occur during the school day.

The best thing you can do is to talk openly and candidly about the loss, make yourself available to your child whenever they wish to discuss the passing of their pet, and not force them to talk about it until he or she is ready to do so. Try to avoid using phrases like "Fluffy was put to sleep" or "Fido went away." Your child may not understand these terms, and phrasing such as this may leave them afraid to fall asleep or unable to understand why their pet suddenly wanted to leave. Saying that the pet "went away" may leave them feeling guilt that something they did led to the pet's passing, which will only serve to distress the child further. Reassure them that the pet's body stopped working, and there was nothing he or she did to cause this. Depending on your faith, you may wish to explain to an older child that the pet's spirit is what made the pet so special; its body merely served as a vessel for the spirit and, in the pet's death, the spirit has departed and looks down upon them always. Be sure your child understands that the pet was lucky to have them in their life. If you recall any funny or happy stories about antics the pet did during life, be sure to remind them of those happy memories. For example, "Do you remember when Shortie grabbed that cupcake off the counter when your brother wasn't watching?" Focusing on the happy memories helps to reframe the sadness.

Don't be afraid to show your own feelings to your child. While, as a parent, you may try to put up a strong front, sometimes it is best to let your child know they are not alone in their grief and that you mourn the loss too. For many families, pets are the equivalent of four-legged family members. Therefore, children – as well as adults – often feel the loss of a pet as strongly as the death of a relative. Be sure to encourage them to open up about their feelings after the loss. Let them know that it is okay to cry, be sad, or talk openly about the pet in its passing. Do not assign blame for the loss of the pet, especially around your children. If you are mourning the pet's death as much as your child, it may be easy to blame the vet for the euthanasia or a relative for accidentally running over your pet. Accidents happen, and euthanasia for an injured or sick animal is the humane way of letting go. Assigning blame only adds more stress to the situation. You are trying to create an atmosphere of calm, peace, and comfort for your child. Children pick up on the stress of others; other pets in the house do as well. The days and weeks after the loss of a pet are trying times; do not make them worse by adding additional, unnecessary stress.

If your child is really struggling, consider writing a letter from the pet to let your child know the pet is happy, grateful for their friendship, and wants the child to keep the memories as they move on with their lives. This can help the child to process that everything will be okay in a way that is non-threatening. Another possibility is to purchase a small piece of memorial jewelry for your child as a way to remember that the love he or she held for their pet is present always.

Talking with your child before and after the loss of a pet, asking your child what you can do to lessen their emotional load, and taking the time to extend some extra tender, loving care will help you to teach them about this fact of life and permit you the opportunity to bond, mourn, and heal together.

ACROSS THE AGES: HOW PET LOSS IMPACTS CHILDREN DURING THEIR YOUNG LIVES

When your child loses his or her pet, a multitude of emotions often rise to the surface. From anger about the fact that the pet has left your child's life, to sadness and loneliness that stem from missing their special friend, children grieve differently depending on their age at the time of the loss. Further, no two children mourn the same way. The emotions felt by one child may be totally different than those experienced by another, and these emotions can and likely will change as the child ages. These challenges may have you, as the parent, asking, "What can I do to help my child through this and any future pet losses?" As you continue reading this book, you will learn how to identify the reactions your child may exhibit after the loss of his or her pet and ways you can help them to deal with the emotions and grief that the death of their pet will create.

Children under the age of two often pick up on the emotions, actions, and conversations of others in the family. If your other children, your significant other, or you are showing emotion or stress around your children as you process the impending end to a pet's life or the loss of the pet itself, your child will likely feel this as well. Children in this age range often struggle with the concept of death because cartoons often depict animated heroes and heroines springing back to life. Your child may not be able to understand why a cartoon character can be severely injured or ill and live, whereas their pet cannot. It is best for you to speak with them in soft, realistic terms about the death of the pet and avoid euphemisms like "Fluffy was put to sleep." Your child may close her doll's eyes and think that's all "put to sleep" means. Short, simple phrasing that is age appropriate will be most beneficial for your child to understand.

Children from ages two to five are more likely to see their pet as a buddy or a living, breathing toy. Children in this age range often struggle with grasping the finality of death. Their young lives have not dealt with loss the way that older children or adults have. They may feel that their pet's passing is fixable or temporary. Further, they may worry that something they did – such as not cleaning their bedroom – may have caused their pet to die. Reverting to previously outgrown habits, such as bed wetting, nail biting, or thumb sucking can return as the child tries to cope with the grief they are experiencing. In the child's need to understand what happened to their special friend, the child may ask questions that may seem out of character, such as "Will Toby have blood coming out his nose?" Also, your child may have difficulty falling or staying asleep because of nightmares about the pet's death, especially if the pet's passing was tragic (run over by a car) or unexpected (the child was not at the vet's office to say goodbye). As the parent, you should ensure your child has access to any resources needed to recover from the loss. If they need therapy to process their grief, search for local counselors trained in helping with grief and loss. Be sure to answer your child's questions truthfully and age-appropriately. Short, simple phrasing to explain that the pet has died and will not be back home will help your child to process this reality. Do not belittle your child's grief or try to rush it to fruition by encouraging them to get over the pet and move on with their lives. Your child will grieve in his or her own time, and you should respect the time your child needs to heal. Lastly, if at all possible, try to say goodbye to the pet – as applicable – before the pet passes.

Children between six and eight years of age are better able to understand the finality of death, though some may feel that death is not permanent. Children in this age range can better understand their own feelings and emotions and, as a result, may feel guilt or anger over the loss of their pet. Your children may feel as though the pet betrayed or abandoned them by leaving and that the pet simply did not care about them anymore. This anger and aggression may occur before or after a sick pet dies. Children this age have a better understanding of what happens when death occurs, but their coping capabilities have not developed to the level of an adult. Therefore, emotions like denial, giving others the silent treatment, or acting normal to avoid facing the magnitude of their grief may be evident.

Changes in your child's eating, sleeping, or playing habits, as well as changes in restroom activities (more or less frequent urination, bowel or bladder control changes), are more likely to occur in this age range. You can help your six-to-eight-year-old child cope with the death of their beloved friend by encouraging them to write their memories of the pet or draw pictures of the pet happily playing with the family. This strengthens the child's good memories of their pet and reframes the grief. Be sure to let your child know their grief is real and totally normal, given the circumstances of the loss. Making sure your child knows that grief and death are facts of life that everyone goes through will help them to know they are not suffering alone and will validate their feelings as normal and realistic. Your child may undertake responsibility for fixing everything, which, of course, they shouldn't. Be sure to explain to your child that they can only control their own emotions, actions, and reactions; the pet's actions and health are not their burden to fix. Because your child is old enough to understand the world around them, it is important that you set a positive atmosphere in motion, even through the sadness, to ensure they can grieve as easily and peacefully as possible. Holding a pet memorial service is a wonderful way for your child to find closure. Involving your child in any pet memorial planning will help them to process the death and honor their friend the way they'd like.

Children between the ages of eight and twelve are equipped to understand death as the end of a life, but lack the ability to accept the pet's passing. While their emotions are in line with the grieving that you or other adults may face, your child may bargain with the pet's loss, feeling maybe if they would clean their room, the pet would return. Children this age are capable of experiencing the gamut of grief stages, from denial and bargaining to anger and guilt. Feelings of depression are also possible before the child reaches the point of accepting that their pal is gone. He or she may attempt to become a family caregiver in order to cling to control of their world. Feelings of independence or acting more grown up as a method to work through their pain can also occur. Children may become antisocial or experience difficulties with their peers or in their homework assignments. They may even miss school due to physical ailments, such as stomach and back pain as depression takes hold. If the child has experienced any losses (e.g., pets, family members) in the past, painful memories or signs of post-traumatic stress disorder may renew. If this happens to your child, professional assistance from a family therapist or grief counselor will be beneficial to helping your child through this rough time. Encourage your children to openly discuss what they are feeling, even if they express their emotions over and over again. This will help them to understand that mourning and grieving are healthy ways to process their pain as opposed to bottling their emotions and withdrawing from the present. If you always make yourself available for your child by offering your comforting ear and warm, parental heart, your child will have a lifeline that will help him or her to heal.

Parents, teachers, and peers often write off a teenager's grief and emotions as unimportant. Many believe these emotions are simply a child "being a teenager." Hormonal changes combined with the confusing emotions surrounding a loss often leave adults struggling to understand the needs of their teen. Withdrawing only worsens the teenager's plight and leaves them hurting and with limited resources to help them cope with their pain. This can lead grieving teens to experiment with other unhealthy choices such as drugs or alcohol. Understandably, these decisions would only serve to make the teen's depression and grieving worse, so it is imperative for you, as the parent, to talk with your teen if a beloved pet has passed. Your child's emotions may be indifferent on the surface, but the pain within may be too much for them to bear. Inevitably, over time, buried emotions will rise to the surface. When they do, your child's emotions will likely explode in either anger or tears. Encourage your child to spend time with his or her friends as isolation can lead to agoraphobia. Whether you seek help from a professional or simply set aside every day to ask your child about his or her feelings, you can help to make a huge difference in your child's life. During the days, weeks, and even months after the loss of a pet, however, try not to judge your child's emotions or decisions. If he or she does not obey all your rules because the grief, cut your child some slack. This time will pass and your child will recover.

Regardless of your child's age or your approach to their healing, the loss of a family pet provides a wonderful opportunity to teach them how to properly and healthily manage their emotions. Those lessons will remain with them for the rest of their lives as they grow and deal with all of life's difficult moments.

IS THE SKY BLUE BECAUSE I'M SAD? QUESTIONS CHILDREN MAY ASK ABOUT PET LOSS

The loss of a pet is a trying time for any family, but young children who are inexperienced in coping with death and understanding the finality of it may ask a multitude of questions ranging from death in general to concerns about their own mortality. This article will share some of the most common questions a child may have after losing a pet and how you may respond to these questions in order to benefit your child's grieving process and learning.

What is death? This is probably the most common question a child may ask and one of the most important for you, as a parent, to ensure your child understands. If your child's pet is the first loss he or she has experienced in their short lives, the concept of death is likely very confusing. It is important for you to explain to your child that death occurs when the body of a pet – or human – no longer works as it should. Explain that your child's veterinarian may have helped the pet in the past, but the pet now suffers from an injury or illness that is too difficult for the pet's body to fight. If the pet is older, be sure your child understands that the aging process changes the body and makes the pet more likely to develop illnesses that drain the body's ability to fight the disease. Sometimes, the body just wears out and cannot bear to fight another day. Your child should hear that dying ultimately results in death to reinforce the finality of such a loss. Depending on your family's cultural or spiritual beliefs, you may wish to explain how the body and spirit differ (e.g., the spirit makes us who we are; the body is just a vessel while we're here on earth).

Was my pet's death my fault? I yelled at him last week for being in the way. Your child may experience guilt over things said or done during the pet's life and worry that they caused the pet's death. Be sure your child understands that death occurs as a result of the body growing tired of fighting an illness or injury and, therefore, it stops working. Death is not caused by anything that your child could say to your pet. Encourage your child to focus on their good memories of their pet and not the moments when they may have been angry at the pet. The memories will last and reframe the child's loss in a positive way.

Why do pets die? A child who sees the world as invincible may not understand why pets must die. Take the time to explain to your child that death is a part of life that eventually happens to us all, because the time we are given on this earth is precious and is not guaranteed. Take this time to help your child see that making the most of each and every day is important, and remind your child that the memories of his or her pet will live on forever.

Will my sadness go away? Your child likely feels very sad about the loss of his or her dear friend. Children who are not yet equipped with the emotional intelligence to absorb that life can be unfair and offers no guarantees may feel as though their suffering will last an eternity. Take this opportunity to extend extra hugs and support to them. Talk about the loss, and explain that grieving is a process that does not happen overnight, within a week, or even a month. Each person mourns differently and at different rates. Be sure they realize that their sadness is normal, but that over time, the pain and sadness will lessen and happiness will return again. Reinforce the message that moving on does not mean forgetting the lost pet; it simply means their memories settle into a comfortable place within your child's heart.

Will I die? Will You Die? The concept of death and the passing of their pet may spark fear in your child. He or she may begin to worry that you or they may soon die too. If the child's pet suffered from an irreversible illness, explaining what happened to their pet may help alleviate some of your child's fears. These fears should always be addressed and never ignored because it is an important life lesson that will help your child deal with any losses later in their lives.

By taking the time to answer each of your child's questions as calmly and compassionately as you can, you will help them process their loss and move on with their lives as quickly as their grief will allow. Should your child feel that they need some way to give their pet a proper goodbye, such as a memorial ceremony, this should be encouraged. It may be beneficial to your children and family if you celebrate the anniversaries of the pet's loss (for the first month or so). Planting a tree or placing a stone in a garden in memory of the pet is also a good way to help them through this difficult time. With a little time and compassion from you, their questions will lessen, and life will return to its new sense of normal.

Dear Teacher, Susie's Pet Passed: Who Needs to be Informed When Your Child Mourns

It is quite understandable that the loss of a pet can cause your child to experience emotions that may not be in their normal character. Your normally quiet child may suddenly begin to act out; your little rebel may become more withdrawn. While no one knows them and what they are experiencing better than you, it is important that other people with whom your child interacts are made aware of why your child's actions may seem out of character so they can assist your child whenever and however possible.

Your child's teachers, coaches, or daycare workers will likely be the first people you need to inform of your child's current emotional state. The loss of a pet may leave your child more likely to resume old habits

– thumb sucking, etc. – and his or her classroom participation may suffer the consequences of an inability to focus due to grief. Since your child spends a great deal of time in daycare or school, their supervisors during this time will be able to help you watch for signs and symptoms of depression or aggression. Further, if your child is typically an honor roll student and suddenly begins to slip into a pattern of turning in work late or incomplete, their teacher will be able to address this with you prior to grades suffering long term. Your child's teacher may be able to help by referring him or her to the school's guidance counselor should his or her grief become unbearable. The educator may also use this time as a lesson for all children, incorporating pet loss topics into the school day, which can assist your child through their period of mourning.

You may wish to inform the parents of your child's friends, as well as your neighbors. If your child performs chores or services for your neighbors (dog walking, babysitting, grass mowing, etc.), you may wish to let your neighbors know that your child is going through a difficult time upon losing their pet and, therefore, their emotions or dedication to the chore may be abnormal. Likewise, your child's friends may not know what to say to assist their friend through their grief. Saying the wrong thing while your child is suffering could lead the best of friends to not see eye to eye. You should inform your child's friends' parents that your child is not on his or her "A" game right now due to grief, so they understand the reasons why.

Depending on your faith, you may wish to let your child's minister or religious leader know about their current state of grief. These faith-based workers often offer support groups and prayers for the grieving. They may also be able to speak with your child and help him or her through their pain.

The loss of a cherished furry, scaly, or feathery friend will likely cause your child to view the world differently than they ever had before their pet passed away. By collaborating with their adult caregivers on the most beneficial ways for the child to process their emotions and move on with their lives, your child will learn the best ways to cope with trauma and be better equipped to handle their grief and the concept of death in the future.

Keep in mind, your other pets can and will mourn loss. Most animals grieve when losing a companion or animal friend. Absence is a feature that pets can feel. Animals such as dogs and cats sense your emotion. They can sense sadness and gloominess, which can cause anxiety or depression. It's best to let them relieve their grief but also play with them just as before. If their irregular behavior becomes destructive, it's best to consult a vet.

MOMMY, I DREW A PICTURE: WAYS TO INVOLVE CHILDREN IN PET MEMORIALS

The emotions that children feel as the result of their beloved pet's passing are often confusing and sad. If your family plans to conduct a memorial service for your pet, there are several ways that you can involve your child in the planning or creation of the remembrance.

When friends and family members share in the mourning process, your child will feel the warmth and love that surrounds them daily. With that in mind, planning a memorial service for their pet that incorporates your child's friends, neighbors, relatives, or classmates will serve two purposes: your child will feel the warmth and love of being surrounded by caring loved ones, and planning the service to incorporate others from your child's inner circle will give your child a chance to create invitations, personalized mementos, or other creative ideas that showcase his or her love for their pet. Their friends and loved ones will offer tremendous respect and surround them with love during the time your child needs it most.

If you have not yet decided, ask for your child's input for the pet's favorite resting spot. This may help you to determine where best to bury the pet or scatter its ashes. Your child may have more insight into the pet's favorite places than you do. Your child may also assist in the creation of a memorial program for the service by writing their thoughts and feelings about the pet or creating drawings that represent the pet through their eyes and recollections. Having them assist in the creation of a pet memorial program offers them the opportunity to release their pent up feelings of anger, sadness, or loneliness and focus on being productive and on the future.

If your family plans to create a pet memorial garden, your child could decorate this location with hand-drawn pictures or stories, or assist you in the decision making surrounding memorial stones or statues. You could ask your child for feedback on any trees, flowers, plants, or bushes you may plant in the garden to honor their special pet's memory.

Some parents choose to help their children remember their lost pets by creating photo collages, scrapbooks, or shadowboxes filled with memories of the dearly departed. Your child could easily get involved in picking which pictures, drawings, etc., to incorporate in a photo collage or scrapbook memorial. My pet memory book, *Memories of You*, is ideal for creating lasting memories and for archiving the relationship your child had with their pet. If your child enjoys writing, you may have them create a story or write poetry honoring their lost pet.

Online memorial websites, such as Pet Memorial http://petmemorial.com, is a free service for grieving pet owners to design and share their most prized memories of their lost pet. Your child could help you pick out pictures for the website or write memories of their beloved friend for the world to read. These websites can be updated as frequently or infrequently as desired. By sharing your child's memories of their pet, you may also be helping others who are mourning their own pet loss.

Creating a plush replica of the pet from a photo is a newer way to remember a lost pet, which may allow your child the opportunity to keep the memories nearby for a long time to come. Companies like Heidi's Custom Plush http://heidiandco.com make stuffed animals from a photo of your child's pet. If you wish to create a custom stuffed animal to help your child through their grief – but not let them know ahead of time – you could seek your child's input by having him or her pick out their favorite picture of their pet. That photograph can be used as the prototype from which a plush replica of the pet is later created.

Whatever you feel is the best way to get your child involved in the process of planning a pet memorial, remember that your main goal should be ensuring that your child's tradition through the stages of grief is as smooth as possible.

MUFFIN'S GONE! WHEN TO MOVE ON?

The decision to replace your dearly departed pet with a new member of the family can be a wonderful way to take a step forward in your healing process, but only when you and your children are ready. Just as there is no timeline for mourning the loss of a human family member, the timeline for moving past the grief of a lost pet is as individual as each person on the planet. For some people, purchasing or adopting a new friend soon after the loss of a pet can help remove the loneliness and emptiness that have set in. However, you must consider the fact that your children may not grieve in the same timetable as you. It is important for you to talk with your kids and allow them the time they need to process and accept the loss before welcoming a new pet into your home. You will be the best gauge of your child's readiness to welcome a new pet into your family. Inevitably, an agreeable child might think he or she is ready to feel that warmth and love again, when realistically, the deeper feelings of sadness speak otherwise. Chances are, if your child is still mentioning your lost pet often or displaying other signs of missing their pet (confusion, anger, remorse, etc.), he or she may not yet be ready.

Children, especially younger kids, often view the world as a place without fear. The traumatic experience of losing a pet may lead to fears that another family member may pass. Further, your child may feel as though their fallen pet is irreplaceable. To ensure that your child does not feel as though a new pet is meant to forget their lost friend, taking the time to consider your options (whether you would want to replace a dog with another dog or another animal completely) and talking with your child at length about their feelings will help you to ensure the time is right for everyone.

When the time comes to adopt or purchase a new family pet, be sure your children understand that the new pet in no way replaces the memories of their dearly departed friend or that pet itself. Your children may struggle to understand this. However, if you approach welcoming a new pet by explaining to your children that their hearts are filled with the love they showed daily to their departed pet and that they have plenty of love to share with a new pet too, you will teach them that love is not a solo emotion, but one that can be shared with many creatures and people. If you find that they are still struggling with fears that their lost pet's memory will be overshadowed by a new four-legged pal, consider hosting a family memorial service for the lost pet to help your child find closure. You could have your child write a short letter to his or her pet, draw pictures of the pet and place them at the headstone or near the pet's favorite resting place, or plant a new tree or flower in memory of your pet.

If you allow your children to take part in the process, such as naming the new pet, picking out the animal, or picking out items for the animal, you will help your child to feel they are an important part in the decision making. This will help them to accept the new addition. Because children are often so attached to their pets, adopting or purchasing a pet of a different breed or gender will help to ensure that your child does not feel their lost buddy is being replaced or forgotten. Adopting a pet that looks too similar to a child's previous pet may lead to disappointment when the child realizes that the new pet acts totally different than their fallen friend. Another option is to forego the pet store and head to your local animal shelter or ASPCA. If your child understands that adopting their new friend from the shelter will save its life, they may realize that while nothing in the world will bring their beloved "Muffin" back, saving a new friend's life and allowing the new pet to enjoy the freedom to roam and live may help your child to move past the pain of losing their old friend.

However you approach welcoming a new pet into your home, remember that there is no timetable on grief, and no two people are alike when it comes to mourning. A timeline that works for your neighbor may not be the timetable for you or your children. Follow your hearts, follow your emotions, and do what is best for your children and your family without regard to what others think. No one knows your needs and those of your children better than you, and when the time to replace your pet is right, everyone in your family will know it.

Conclusion

The loss of a pet is an unfortunate circumstance that all pet owners eventually have to face. Grieving is a common feature of that loss. Although, we refer to our furry friends as pets, most of us think of them as members of the family. With love and loss come a lot of tears and confusion. And while people deal with grief differently, there are a few things that are most often neglected as the grief clouds your mind. I hope by offering these tips and advice, your child's burden of pet loss can be eased and the healing process can begin.

10 Most Asked Questions When Dealing With Pet Loss

1. How do I tell my children about the loss of our pet?

Despite what people may think, children have the right to know about the loss of their pet. As a parent, it is up to you to determine how much information to convey to your child. For some parents death is much too morbid for their children to understand, so it is best to be mild when explaining what happened. Start with the negative and sad, but end with a positive statement. For example, "While our pet is no longer here with us, think about all the great memories that you still have." This statement conveys the sad truth but offers a positive explanation to ease the grief that may develop as they realize the extent of this loss.

2. What if I tell my children they "went away?"

I recommend that you do not sugar coat or completely lie. Most often, sugar-coated explanations contain more grief than honesty. For example, by telling your child the pet has "gone away," you are causing the child to believe that it is coming back. And if you tell your child that he is asleep, you are inserting a level of hope that the pet will one day wake up. Both will create grief and a level of mistrust when the truth is identified. Remember, you don't have to explain every detail, but explain the scenario so that they understand the nature of losing their pet.

3. Should I grieve?

Mourning is a feature that comes with the loss of something you love. There isn't anything that can measure that love despite what people may say. Your pet may have been another species, but it gave you unconditional love and was part of the family. Just like with humans, you should grieve and cry as you remember the loss of your friend. While I can't tell you how to deal with your feelings, I can definitely advise that you don't hold them in. Burying your feelings can make the grief last much longer, and trying to ignore how you feel can make the pain feel much worse.

4. Should I grieve in front of my children?

Yes! Grieve in front of your children so they do not feel shame by how sad they are about the circumstances of their furry friend. The phrase, "monkey see monkey do" has never been more relevant than now. If they see you grieving, then they will feel more comfortable grieving themselves. You want to convey the message that grieving is typical. It may be an irregular trait when Dad grieves the loss of their pet, but seeing him grieve can make it more comfortable and normal. Note that stigmatizing sensitivity in this scenario is a complete no-no. Chastising someone for crying is *never* acceptable, especially when death is involved.

5. What can help ease the grief?

Whatever way feels most comfortable to you and those who are suffering with you. Some people like to celebrate the life of the pet rather than grieve the loss. You can also create a memorial in a section of the house, a place where there are pictures of all the good times. Crying and venting are common features of grief; they relieve some of the feelings that are present after you've lost your friend. Ultimately, grieving is a relative feature that will happen at different times and will affect each person differently. As long as it isn't destructive to you or anybody else, it is safe to grieve the way you want. I recommend confiding in someone about your loss and remembering the good times that made you love and laugh with your pet.

Crying for someone you love never makes you a weak person; everyone has the right to grieve no matter who or what they've lost.

6. What resources are available to help the family grieve?

There are so many resources available for those who deal with pet loss grief. Friends, extended family, co-workers, and colleagues can help with the grief. It's also a good idea to explain the situation to the teachers of your younger children. The loss of a pet will definitely affect the children's school routine during the first parts of the morning process.

7. Should We Give The Pet a Funeral?

It depends on what works for you and your family. For some, a funeral is the only way to honor their friend. Take the children's wants into consideration. If the children want to have a funeral, then do so to relieve the grieving. You want to satisfy everyone's wants within reason. It also depends on the role your pet played in the family. You don't have to give a funeral for every snake or goldfish that your family loses. Of course, in the end, animals are an important feature of the family life; what matters to you and your family should all be taken into consideration.

8. What should I do with the remains?
There are several options when handling the pet's remains. You can have a burial site for the pet in the family yard. Just like with human loss, children like to visit the burial site to speak with their friend. Take into account the city regulations of a home burial. It is not recommended for those who rent or share property with others.

You can also bury them at a pet cemetery. This is the most costly option, but it may satisfy the family to know the pet is being buried with honor as a family member rather than being treated like a regular animal. It's also an option for those who are renters.

You can cremate the animal. Very few places specialize in this feature, but it is possible for a pet to be cremated. It may be the better option for those who need the physical form but don't want to go as far as taxidermy.

9. How soon should I get a new pet?
Simple. When you're ready. Choosing a pet is the same no matter how many pets you've lost. When you are ready to give a new pet the love and attention it needs, then you are ready. If you still feel as though you are too sad to show your new pet love, then you may want to wait a while. With any pet you want to make sure you can take care of it, physically as well as emotionally. It's also better to think of this pet as a new friend rather than as a replacement. Just like with people, each pet has its own identity. You don't want to compare and contrast, and you don't want to give

them the same name as the pet you've lost. That's too much pressure on the pet and the family.

10. What about the other pets? Do they grieve?

Yes. Most animals grieve when losing a companion or animal friend. Absence is a feature that can be felt from pets, and as they notice, this absence grief will take place. Animals such as dogs and cats sense your emotion. They can sense sadness and gloominess, which can cause anxiety or depression. It is best to let them relieve their grief but also play with them just as before. If their irregular behavior becomes destructive, it is best to consult a veteran.

MEET THE AUTHOR

Author | **Erainna Winnett, Ed. S.**

Erainna was born and raised in central Louisiana. The oldest of five children she always yearned to be a teacher and forced her siblings to play school year round. Naturally, she graduated with a teaching degree in 1995 and earned her Master's degree in 2000. Five years later she earned her Education Specialist degree in early childhood education. After fifteen years in the classroom, she moved to the role of school counselor and has never been happier.

While serving as school counselor at an elementary school in north Texas, she frequently uses picture books as therapy to help her students heal, learn, and grow. Ideas for her books come from the students she works with on a daily basis. Her goal, as an author, is to touch the hearts of children, one story at a time.

An avid animal lover Erainna lives on a 300 acre cattle ranch near the Red River with her husband, two daughters, three dogs, two horses, and one ill-tempered cat.

ALSO BY ERAINNA WINNETT, ED. S.

**THERAPEUTIC ACTIVITY BOOKS
Helping Kids Heal Series**
Each engaging, interactive activity book, written to address a specific topic, is designed to guide children during their most troubled times and allows them to process their pain through art therapy, self-reflection, and self-awareness activities. (ages 6-16)

Beyond Being Bullied (resiliency)
Somebodyness (self-confidence)
Outsmart Test Anxiety (test anxiety)
Chill Out (anger management)
Mom or Dad's House (divorce)
Twice the Love (blended family)
Broken Promises (disappointment)
A Brighter Tomorrow (trauma)
Cyber Savvy (cyberbullying)
Saying Goodbye (memory book)
Memories of You (pet memory book)

MIDDLE SCHOOL GUIDES FOR TWEENS (6x9, 128 pages each)
Tween Talk: A Tween's Guide to SOCIAL SUCCESS
Tween Time: A Tween's Guide to ACADEMIC SUCCESS

PICTURE BOOKS
Girl Power: Believe in Yourself Series
It's Good to Be Me
Frenemy Jungle
Friendship Tug-of-War
Cyber Friend?

Making a Difference Series
The Bully Trap
Superheroes: The Power of the Bystander
Winter Wishes: A Story of Compassion
Mathsketball: A Story of Test Anxiety
New School, New Friends

Where to connect with Erainna...

http://erainnawinnett.com

http://counselingwithheart.com